THE APPALACHIANS

CHARLES W. MAYNARD

The Rosen Publishing Group's
PowerKids Press™
New York

For Caroline and Jamie, who are beginning their lives together in the Appalachians. And for the Cumberlands and the Great Smokies, my mountain homes.

Published in 2004 by The Rosen Publishing Group, Inc.
29 East 21st Street, New York, NY 10010

First Edition

Editor: Frances E. Ruffin
Book Design: Emily Muschinske
Photo Researcher: Barbara Koppleman

Photo Credits: Cover and p. 1 © Randy Wells/Getty Images; pp. 4, 11 (bottom) © Maria Stenzell/National Geographic Image Collection; p. 7 © Randy Olson/Getty Images; p. 7 (inset) © 2002 Geoatlas; p. 8 © Vanessa Vick/Photo Researchers; p. 8 (inset) © Gilbert & Grant/Photo Researchers; p. 11 (top) © Phil Schermeister/CORBIS; p. 12 © Carr Clifton/Minden Pictures; p. 15 (bottom) © Robert Lubeck/Animals Animals; p. 15 (top) © Raymond K. Gehman/National Geographic Image Collection; p. 16 © Roger Ressmeyer/CORBIS; p. 19 © Bettmann/CORBIS; p. 19 (inset) © North Wind Picture Archives; p. 20 © David Meunch/CORBIS.

Maynard, Charles W. (Charles William), 1955–
The Appalachians / Charles W. Maynard.—1st ed.
    v. cm.— (Great mountain ranges of the world)
Includes bibliographical references (p.) and index.
Contents: Mountains of the Eastern United States—Ancient mountains—A rocky past—A cool, wet climate—A variety of plants—Animals large and small—Appalachian industries—Exploring rugged mountains—A rich mountain heritage—The Appalachian Trail.
  ISBN 0-8239-6695-X
1. Appalachian Mountains—Juvenile literature. [1. Appalachian Mountains. 2. Mountains.] I. Title.
  F106 .M49 2004
  917.4—dc21

                                                                    2002013502

Manufactured in the United States of America

CONTENTS

MOUNTAINS OF THE EASTERN UNITED STATES

The Appalachian Mountains make up an **ancient** mountain chain that stretches more than 1,500 miles (2,414 km), across the length of eastern North America. The range begins in Newfoundland, Canada, and runs south and west to the state of Alabama.

The Appalachians are not tall mountains compared to the Rockies in the western United States, or the Himalayas in Asia. **Altitudes** in the Appalachians vary from 1,500 feet (475 m) to the highest peak, on Mount Mitchell in North Carolina, at 6,684 feet (2,037 m). The Alleghenies of New York, the White Mountains of New Hampshire, the Blue Ridge of Virginia and North Carolina, and the Great Smoky Mountains of Tennessee and North Carolina are some of the ranges that make up the Appalachians. Much of the Appalachian region is known for its **fertile** valleys with farmlands and forest-covered mountains. Many great rivers, such as the Hudson, Ohio, Shenandoah, and Tennessee Rivers, begin as mountain streams, swollen by rainfall.

◀ *A dairy farmer harvests corn in the Catskill chain of the Appalachian mountains. Spanish explorer Hernando de Soto named the mountains for the Appalachee Indians.*

ANCIENT MOUNTAINS

The Appalachians are old mountains. Some of the rock in them formed from 750 million to 1 billion years ago. Large slabs of rock called **plates** make up Earth's **crust**. Over millions of years these plates have slowly moved, bumped into one another, and caused huge wrinkles in the crust. The wrinkles became mountains. These types of mountains are called fold mountains, because they folded up when the plates collided, or bumped into each other. The Appalachians were made by plates colliding over millions of years. The last collision occurred more than 200 million years ago. Each time the mountains were pushed up, ice, water, and wind have worked to wear them down. This **erosion** created steep mountainsides and deep valleys. The Appalachians are slowly becoming worn away, sending **sediment** by river to the Atlantic Ocean and the Gulf of Mexico.

MOUNTAIN

THE GREAT SMOKY MOUNTAINS ARE GOOD EXAMPLES OF EROSION IN ACTION. SOMETIMES HEAVY SUMMER THUNDERSTORMS CAUSE LANDSLIDES THAT PUSH DOWN TREES AND EXPOSE ROCK. THESE LARGE SCARS OF EXPOSED ROCK IN THE GREAT SMOKIES ARE CALLED BALDS.

FACT

The Great Smokies are in Tennessee. Inset: The map shows the complete Appalachian mountain range in the Eastern United States and Canada.

Lake Superior

Québec

Montréal

OTTAWA

St Lawrence

Fredericton

Lake Huron

Montpelier

Augusta

Nova

Toronto

Lake Ontario

Portland

waukee

Lansing

Lake Erie

Buffalo

Albany

Boston

Lake Michigan

Detroit

Cleveland

Hartford

Providence

Chicago

Pittsburgh

New York

Philadelphia

ianapolis

Columbus

Baltimore

Ohio

Charleston

WASHINGTON

-Louis

Frankfort

APPALACHIAN MOUNTAINS

Richmond

Norfolk

Nashville

Tennessee

Raleigh

irmingham

Charlotte

Atlanta

Columbia

Charleston

son

Montgomery

Bermuda
UK

Mobile

Tallahassee

New
Orleans

FLORIDA

Tampa

Miami

NASSAU

A ROCKY PAST

The Appalachians are made of three types of rock. Sedimentary rock begins as small pieces of rock and soil that are carried by water, ice, or wind, and that are left at the bottom of a sea. Layers of sediment harden and become rock. Chalk and **limestone** are forms of sedimentary rock. These rocks may contain plant **fossils** and the shells of tiny sea animals. Some Appalachian mountains have igneous rock, which was formed when extremely hot **magma**, forced from below Earth's surface, hardened. Granite and basalt are two kinds of igneous rock. Metamorphic rock makes up part of the range. It was formed when sedimentary or igneous rock was subjected to extreme heat and pressure during the mountain-building process. Each type of rock is found in different parts of the range, depending on the age of the mountain. For instance, there are no fossils in the Blue Ridge or Great Smoky Mountains. They were created before creatures were large enough to leave fossils. Over time, fossils produced coal, oil, and natural gas.

The Luray Caverns, in Virginia, are part of the Appalachians. Many stalactites and stalagmites, or the natural rock columns that extend from the ceilings and floors, decorate the cave. Inset: These limestone fossils were found in the North Carolina Appalachians.

A Cool, Wet Climate

The **climate** of the Appalachian Mountains depends on their **elevation**. On a hot summer's day in the Great Smokies, where some peaks reach 6,500 feet (1,981 m), the **temperatures** can range from nearly 100°F (38°C), in the foothills, to a cooler 78°F (26°C) on a mountain peak.

The higher peaks of the Appalachians receive more rain than the valleys do. Some mountains receive up to 100 inches (254 cm) of rain each year while surrounding lower areas only get 50 inches (127 cm). Few regions in the Appalachians have weather as severe as New Hampshire's Mt. Washington. Its highest peak is the coldest and receives the most snow of the entire range. Most mountain regions have longer, colder winters and shorter, cooler summers. Snow remains on the peaks into the month of May.

MOUNTAIN FACT

WHERE IS THE WORST WEATHER IN THE WORLD? MT. WASHINGTON, 6,288 FEET (1,917 M) IN NEW HAMPSHIRE, HAS AN AVERAGE ANNUAL SNOWFALL OF 256 INCHES (650 CM). WINDS THERE ARE STRONGER THAN HURRICANE FORCE AT 75 MPH (121 KM/H), FOR ABOUT 104 DAYS EACH YEAR, AND WINDS RECORDED AT 231 MPH (372 KM/H).

A boater enjoys a sunny day in New York's Adirondack Mountains. Top: Mt. Washington's icy slopes are a favorite place for mountain climbers.

A VARIETY OF PLANTS

The last ice age occurred about 10,000 years ago. Its **glaciers** wiped out many plant **species** in the Appalachians. However, many species lived through the freeze. Today more than 2,000 plant species grow in the Appalachians. What types of plants grow in the different regions of these mountains depends on altitude, rainfall, temperature, and the length of the growing season.

Evergreen **conifers**, such as pines and fir trees, grow in the northern Appalachians and on some of the highest peaks in the South. A mixture of hardwood trees, such as oak, hickory, poplar, beech, maple, hemlock, and white pine, grow in the South and on slopes in lower elevations. More than 130 species of trees grow in the Great Smoky Mountains' high peaks and low river valleys. Many people travel throughout the different Appalachian regions to see the wildflowers in spring and the changing colors of the tree leaves in the autumn.

The Blue Ridge Mountains of George Washington National Forest in Virginia are known for their beautiful autumn leaves.

Animals Large and Small

Many creatures, both large and small, live in the Appalachian mountains. More than 200 species of bird spend at least part of each year in the mountains of the region. Many birds, such as the scarlet tanager, live and breed in the Appalachians, but spend winters in South America. Other birds, such as the junco, spend summers high in the mountains. They nest in valleys during cold weather. From Maine to Georgia, the Appalachians are home to the white-tailed deer and the black bear. Deer live in great numbers in the hilly areas of the mountains that have both fields and forests. Black bears live in the forests. The elk, a large member of the deer family, once lived in many parts of the mountains. In the 1800s, elk were hunted for their meat until they disappeared from the region. Elk are now being brought back into the mountains in Pennsylvania, Kentucky, Tennessee, and North Carolina.

MOUNTAIN FACT

Black bears eat berries, acorns, insects, and fish. A black bear can eat as much as 45 pounds (20 kg) of food and can gain up to 5 pounds (2.5 kg) per day as it prepares to hibernate, or sleep. It sleeps for up to seven months when it is cold and there is little food. Black bears live from 10 to 25 years.

A male scarlet tanager feeds his nestlings.
Top: A black bear cub looks for food in the Great Smoky Mountains.

APPALACHIAN INDUSTRIES

The U.S. government describes Appalachia as an area covering 406 counties in 13 states. For **geographers,** it covers 16 states and a **province** in Canada.

For centuries, Native Americans and European settlers lived in the hidden valleys of the rugged mountains. These people preferred to farm in their quiet valleys and to hunt for game in the forested mountains. Then, in the late 1800s, **resources** in the region were in great demand for the nation's growing industries, or businesses. Coal was mined to run factories, and trees were harvested for **timber**. Railroads, and eventually highways and airports, brought an end to **isolation** in much of the region. Today coal mining, timber, and **tourism** are three of the area's major industries.

Concern for the **environment** has slowed the amount of mining and timbering. The scenic beauty of the mountains attracts millions of visitors each year. Shenandoah National Park, Great Smoky Mountains National Park, and Blue Ridge Parkway are three of the many federal parks set aside to protect the natural resources.

◀ *A mining machine called a logwall shearer cuts out large chunks of coal at the Blacksville mine in Wana, West Virginia.*

EXPLORING RUGGED MOUNTAINS

The earliest recorded **exploration** of the Appalachians was made by the Spaniard Hernando de Soto in the 1540s. Later, when European settlers thought of moving west from the East, the Appalachians made travel difficult. Few people traveled beyond the mountains. In 1750, Dr. Thomas Walker led an **expedition** through a narrow pass, or trail, in the Cumberland Mountains. He named the pass the Cumberland Gap. In 1773, Daniel Boone, an **explorer** and a fur trapper, led several families through the gap to settle in Kentucky. Two years later, Boone and a group of 30 men widened the trail and built the Wilderness Road. By the end of the 1700s, thousands of people had taken the Wilderness Road through the Cumberland Gap to settle in Kentucky and Tennessee.

MOUNTAIN FACT

In the Great Smoky mountains National Park, scientists are still discovering new species of plants and animals in the Appalachian region. Some scientists think that there may be more than 100,000 species of life in the Park. This effort may take from 10 to 12 years to complete.

Early Americans traveled west through the Cumberland Gap. Inset: In 1540, Hernando de Soto met the Cofitachequi Indians in the southern Appalachians.

THE APPALACHIAN TRAIL

The Appalachian National Scenic Trail is a path once used by Native Americans. It winds 2,144 miles (3,450 km) southward from Mount Katahdin in Maine to Springer Mountain in Georgia. Benton MacKaye, a forest planner, first proposed the idea for a long Appalachian trail in 1921. Volunteers, or people who worked without pay, completed the trail for hikers in 1937. Volunteers have cared for it since then. It passes through 14 states, 8 national forests, and 2 national parks.

A hiker who walks the entire Appalachian Trail in one season, from March to October, is called a through-hiker. Most people walk only a part of this long trail. No matter how far people walk along the Appalachian Trail, they experience the beauty of the mountains. They also experience the richness of plant and animal life, and the wonder of Appalachian culture in different regions. Although coal mining, timbering, and erosion have stripped the mountains in many places, many people are working to solve these problems to keep the Appalachian Mountains beautiful.

This beautiful view of the Appalachian National Scenic Trail is part of Brown's Gap, Shenandoah National Park, Virginia.

A Rich Mountain Heritage

Appalachia is a land of great storytellers. The Cherokee tell a story of Grandfather Buzzard to explain how the mountains were formed. The Cherokee believed that, when the world began, all the land was mud surrounded by water. The animals wanted to live on the land but they did not want to live in the mud. Grandfather Buzzard offered to flap his huge wings to dry the mud and make the land into hard ground. There was so much land that he got tired. As he tired, he flew lower and lower. His huge wings dug out deep valleys and lifted up the mountains. The Cherokee called the mountains The Land Where Buzzard Tired.

The Appalachian region is also known for its **heritage** of storytelling and the music of the people who settled there. Many of those settlers were Scotch-Irish people. They brought their stories and music with them and passed these arts down to their children and grandchildren. The National Storytelling Festival is held each year in Jonesborough, Tennessee. Many other festivals and museums throughout the region help to save the Appalachian heritage for future generations.

GLOSSARY

altitudes (AL-tih-toodz) Heights above Earth's surface.

ancient (AYN-chent) Very old; from a long time ago.

climate (KLY-mit) The kind of weather a certain area has.

conifers (KAH-nih-furz) Trees that have needlelike leaves and grow cones.

crust (KRUST) The outer, or top, layer of a planet.

elevation (eh-luh-VAY-shun) The height of an object.

environment (en-VY-urn-ment) All the living things and conditions of a place.

erosion (ih-ROH-shun) The wearing away of land over time.

expedition (ek-spuh-DIH-shun) A trip for a special purpose, such as scientific study.

exploration (ek-spluh-RAY-shun) Traveling through little-known land.

explorer (ik-SPLOR-ur) A person who travels and looks for new land.

fertile (FUR-tul) Good for making and growing things.

fossils (FA-sulz) The hardened remains of a dead animal or plant that lived long ago.

geographers (jee-AH-gruh-ferz) Scientists who study the features of Earth.

glaciers (GLAY-shurz) Large masses of ice that move down a mountain or along a valley.

heritage (HER-ih-tij) The stories and ways of doing things that are handed down from parent to child.

isolation (eye-suh-LAY-shun) Being apart or alone.

limestone (LYM-stohn) A kind of rock made of the bodies of small ocean animals.

magma (MAG-muh) A hot, liquid rock underneath Earth's surface.

plates (PLAYTS) The moving pieces of the Earth's crust.

province (PRAH-vins) One of the main parts of a country.

resources (REE-sors-es) A supply or a source of energy or useful materials.

sediment (SEH-dih-mint) Gravel, sand, silt, or mud that is carried by wind or water.

species (SPEE-sheez) A single kind of plant or animal. All people are one species.

temperatures (TEM-pruh-cherz) How hot or cold something is.

timber (TIM-bur) Wood that is cut and used for building houses, ships, and other objects.

tourism (TUR-ih-zem) A business that deals with people who travel for pleasure.

Index

Web Sites

Due to the changing nature of Internet links, PowerKids Press has developed an online list of Web sites related to the subject of this book. This site is updated regularly. Please use this link to access the list:

www.powerkidslinks.com/gmrw/appalach/